D1607037

ANTARCTIC WILDLIFE

BY JAMES BUCKLEY JR.

EXPLORING THE POLAR REGIONS TODAY

ANTARCTIC WILDLIFE

BY JAMES BUCKLEY, JR.

MASON CREST

Mason Crest
450 Parkway Drive, Suite D
Broomall, PA 19008
www.masoncrest.com

© 2018 by Mason Crest, an imprint of National Highlights, Inc.

Printed and bound in the United States of America.

First printing
1 3 5 7 9 8 6 4 2

Series ISBN: 978-1-4222-3863-9
ISBN: 978-1-4222-3864-6
ebook ISBN: 978-1-4222-7919-9

Library of Congress Cataloging-in-Publication Data on file with the publisher.

Developed and Produced by Shoreline Publishing Group.
Developmental Editor: James Buckley, Jr.
Design: Tom Carling, Carling Design Inc.
Production: Sandy Gordon
www.shorelinepublishing.com
Front cover: Dreamstime.com/Jan Martin Will.

QR Codes disclaimer:

CONTENTS

Key Icons to Look For

Words to Understand: These words with their easy-to-understand definitions will increase the reader's understanding of the text, while building vocabulary skills.

Sidebars: This boxed material within the main text allows readers to build knowledge, gain insights, explore possibilities, and broaden their perspectives by weaving together additional information to provide realistic and holistic perspectives.

Educational Videos: Readers can view videos by scanning our QR codes, providing them with additional educational content to supplement the text. Examples include news coverage, moments in history, speeches, iconic moments, and much more!

Text-Dependent Questions: These questions send the reader back to the text for more careful attention to the evidence presented here.

Research Projects: Readers are pointed toward areas of further inquiry connected to each chapter. Suggestions are provided for projects that encourage deeper research and analysis.

Series Glossary of Key Terms: This back-of-the-book glossary contains terminology used throughout this series. Words found here increase the reader's ability to read and comprehend higher-level books and articles in this field.

INTRODUCTION

Winter temperatures well below freezing…nothing but ice for thousands of miles . . . icy cold water that would test the strongest wet suit …a landscape nearly empty of plants. Who—or what—would want to live in a place like that?

That place is Antarctica, the south-ernmost continent and site of the South Pole. Its vast landmass is nearly entirely covered in ice year-round, yet somehow life does win the battle to survive. On its icy slopes, along rocky coastlines, and on craggy islands un-der assault from high winds, animals battle the elements to thrive. In the waters around Antarctica, including the treacherous South Atlantic Ocean, more animal life teems, from enormous whales to microscopic plankton.

Though most of the Antarctic re-gion is ice, it is the waters of the ocean that provide most of the habitats for wildlife. In fact, the ice of the main body of the Antarctic continent is so cold and forbidding, nearly all animals only visit there in the slightly warmer summer. The largest animal that lives year-round in Antarctica is barely larg-er than the period at the end of this sentence. You can meet it on page 41.

The key to life in Antarctica and the islands around it is adaptation. That is the process through which a species, via evolution across thousands of years, becomes the right animal for its home. In the case of animals of Antarctica and its surrounding seas, being able to handle extreme cold is the most important adaptation. Some animals do this with body parts such as blubber. Others use hiberna-tion—"shutting down" their bodies during the harshest weather.

Along with body adaptations, they must be able to find the right food. The food chain in the Antarctic eco-system is very interdependent. That means that each link in the chain is vital to the success of the entire chain. Whales depend on tiny krill; seals, penguins, and birds depend on fish. The krill and fish depend on plankton and smaller animals. And the waters themselves help provide plant plankton that feeds the krill, starting the cycle around again.

Because of the fragile nature of this chain, scientists are watching Antarctica carefully. Global climate change is bringing new challenges to the animals of this region. The

Local residents of the Antarctic, including penguins, are being increasingly threatened by human visitors and the effects of human-created climate change.

temperature of the water is changing, meaning that animals living there once again have to adapt. Their success at that process will determine the future of this vital food chain. In addition, human beings are having direct effects, such as through overfishing of some species.

The good news is that while many animals have adapted to survive in these difficult areas, humans have not. There is little human settlement in Antarctica. The massive impacts of development and civilization that have affected wild areas around the world have not clashed too much with this southern continent. There are some small settlements on Antarctic islands, and several nations take part in scientific research stations on the continental mainland. But so far at least, a massive invasion of the human species has been slowed by the devastating cold and the mighty winds. Is nature working hard to keep people out? Or will people find a way to get in here? This book is a look at the animals that live in this icy wilderness, animals who are hoping the answer to that last question is no.

This Weddell seal pup shows the characteristic thick fur of its species. That fur was the target of hunters until conservationists rallied to help slow the practice.

Marine Mammals

1

Words to Understand

apex predator   an animal that has no natural predators in its habitat and is also the top hunter of other animals in the area

dorsal   attached to the spine or back of an animal, usually an aquatic one

food web   the interconnected group of animals that feed on and off each other

theorize   use evidence to create a reasonable conclusion about a question

The icy waters and forbidding rocky coasts of Antarctica and its nearby islands test the toughest of creatures. Yet one group has thrived there, thanks to adaptations that make it their perfect home. The large variety of marine mammals is at the top of the **food web** of the Antarctic. They are among the few types of animals that use both the land—for breeding and resting—and the sea, where they spend most of their time and which provides nearly all their food.

Marine mammals—whales, seals, walruses, and others—breathe air like other mammals. They must surface on a regular basis to take in air before once more diving into their watery homes. Like all mammals, they give birth to live young and keep them nearby as the young feed from the mother. And though it doesn't look like it from their sleek skins, whales do have a small amount of hair, usually near their mouths or eyes. Some marine mammals, such as seals or walruses, have hairy pelts, or outer skins.

Top of the Chain

When it's winter in the Northern Hemisphere, it's summer around Antarctica. That's the season when whales are most plentiful. The waters are still near freezing, but the air temperatures are not as bitterly cold as in the winter.

At the top of the Antarctic food web as the **apex predators** are the killer whales, or orcas. Killer whales are actually part of the dolphin family, recognizable by their single **dorsal** fin and torpedo-shaped bodies. Typically they are mostly black with white patches. During their time in chilly southern waters, some species also have coatings of yellowish plankton on parts of their bodies.

Killer whales stay at the top of the food chain thanks to their speed, power, and intelligence. About 16–25 feet (4.8–7.6 m) long, they have huge, fierce jaws lined with sharp teeth. Their prey is just about anything moving in the sea, from fish to seals to whales. They are among the few animals in the world that practice cooperative hunting. For example, one whale will rise up near a

Orcas typically move in groups called pods. This not only creates a community for raising young, but also they can work together in hunting behaviors.

small ice floe and smack into it, sending a resting seal into the water. There, other whales in the pack can chase and eat it. The first whale probably won't get any, but he'll get his turn. When attacking a much larger humpback or blue whale, the killer whales act as a pack, attacking until the prey is subdued enough for all to feed. Video of individual killer whales pursuing seals onto rocky beaches demonstrates these predators will to do anything to catch their prey. In the Antarctic, biologists have named three major types of orcas based on their feeding behavior. "A" orcas focus on minke (MINN-kee) whales; "B" orcas on seals; and "C" orcas on toothfish and other fish.

Penguins are a key prey species for some types of killer whales. The huge number of the birds in the Antarctic draws one of the world's largest orca gatherings.

Like many other whales, orcas communicate using sounds. Clicks, pulses, and whistling noises can be heard underwater as the killer whales move together. Scientists **theorize** that the sounds are directions on working together.

Because they were never hunted for food or oil, killer whales have not faced any significant level of danger from humans. They also have no natural enemies in the water. However, human impact on the oceans—from pollution to rising temperatures due to climate change—will have a long-term negative effect on these mighty beasts.

Antarctic Whales

Much, much larger than killer whales, but almost completely harmless to other mammals is the blue whale. The Antarctic species of blue whale is probably the largest animal ever to live on the earth. Blues can be more than 80 feet (24 m) long and weigh an estimated 300,000 pounds (136,000 kg). Yet they eat only tiny shrimp and krill or small fish. Blue whales' mouths contain huge sheets of a strong, thin material called baleen. Hanging in strips inside the jaws, the baleen acts as a sieve or a strainer. The whale gulps huge mouthfuls of water. As the water passes through the

Even though blue whales are so enormous, this is the most that can usually be seen—the blowhole as the whale surfaces to breathe.

baleen, tiny animals are caught and sent to the whale's stomach; the water passes out of the whale again.

Humpback whales are found in many places around the world, but many of them spend some time each year in Antarctic waters. Like blues, they are filter feeders that use baleen. Humpbacks have been famous for their communication skills. Scientists have recorded these whales using sounds that seems to be signals to other humpbacks. There are different kinds of calls, or songs, for different situations. Some experts theorize that humpbacks can identify individuals from their songs, too.

This humpback is demonstrating the filter feeding behavior. Its huge mouth sucks in seawater—fish, krill, and all—and its baleen takes the fish and releases the water.

Humpbacks and sperm whales can be identified by their unique tail flukes. When they dive after breathing, as shown here, it is called "sounding."

If you see a sperm whale in the Antarctic, it's a male. Females and young sperm whales stay farther north year-round, where the water is warmer. In the southern summer, however, male sperm whales can be seen around the Antarctic. They can be as long as 40 feet (12 m) and weigh an estimated 32,000 pounds (14,500 kg). Sperm whales are toothed whales, with long rows of large teeth on both jaws. Squid are among their main foods, and several species of humpbacks flourish in the nutrient-rich waters of the south.

The smaller, shyer minke whales are among the most threatened in the area. Scientists report that numbers of these marine mammals have fallen sharply.

Minke whales also summer in the Antarctic for both feeding and breeding. They are the smallest of the baleen whales at about 25–30 feet (7.6–9.1 m) and about 20,000 pounds (9,000 kg). Minkes are some of the fastest whales, too. They use that speed to chase swarms of krill, their main diet, or to avoid orcas, for whom they are prey. The number of minke whales is falling fast, however. Scientists are closely watching this species to find out the reasons for the decline.

However, another species is doing very well in the southern waters. Humpback whale populations are actually going up. They need wide areas of open ocean to pursue the krill on which they feed. In an ironic twist, the reduction of the sea ice has made more room for these huge, singing mammals.

Sei whales are very large baleen whales that live part of the year in the Antarctic. Males can be more than 60 feet (18.2 m) long and weigh more than 100,000 pounds (45,000 kg). They are rarely seen partly because their world population numbers are low and partly because they do not make a big display when diving beneath the waves. They were not heavily hunted until the 1950s, when declining numbers of other whales made them a target. Recovery efforts, however, have helped their numbers return to nearly healthy levels.

The creation of the Ross Sea Marine Protected Area could help some of these whale populations increase.

Antarctic Seals

While whales are tourists in the area for the nice weather, seals and sea lions of several species make their year-round home in the Antarctic.

Leopard seals take their name from the dark spots on parts of their pelt. The name is also inspired by their fierce attacking style and sharp teeth. Leopard seals are some of the deadliest predators of penguins.

If crabeater seals actually had to eat only crabs, they'd go rather hungry in the Antarctic. There are relatively few crab species, certainly not enough to feed the estimated 15 million crabeaters

This is a penguin's worst nightmare: the deadly teeth of the leopard seal. Those powerful jaws and sharp fangs can quickly turn a bird into a meal.

that live here. Crabeaters eat mostly krill, another crustacean and the source of their German-inspired name, *krebs*. They are one of three seal species to spend their whole lives in and around the pack ice surrounding the continent.

Elephant seals are a migratory species. These enormous marine mammals—adult males can be more than 6,600 pounds (3000 kg)—spend the southern winter on icy Antarctic birthing grounds, returning in spring to feed and breed. They haul their huge bulks onto ice shelves and rocky shores for breeding, often on islands near the Antarctic mainland. The males are famous for their displays of temper when battling for their mates. They clash together, chest to chest, while slashing with sharp teeth and emitting very loud bellows. Elephant seals can dive great depths in search of food, perhaps more than 5,000 feet (1500 m), but they are very clumsy on land, as might be expected for such huge animals. They get their name not from their size but from the large flap of skin and tissue on the front of their head. It includes their nose parts and is known as a proboscis. It lets the males emit loud bellows that can be heard for miles. The sounds are used to impress mates and threaten rivals.

Weddell seals get their name from the Weddell Sea, a part of the Southern Ocean alongside Antarctica. They stay farther south than any other mammals, swimming most often right along the edge of the ice. They can also swim under fast-ice, which is frozen seawater, and dig out air holes with sharp teeth. A smaller species is named for the Ross Sea. Not as much is known about this shy, and more rare, species, but it, too, has sharp teeth to snag quick-moving fish.

All seals are mammals, of course, so they have some hair, such as whiskers. Fur seals, however, have hairy pelts all over their bodies. This has made them attractive over the centuries to hunters. Today, hunting them is illegal, so the animals live safely on some of the small islands around the Antarctic continent. The males can be fairly large, up to 440 pounds (200 kg), while females are only about a third that size.

This southern elephant seal shows off the huge nose that is the source of its name. The animals are the largest species of seal in the world.

From enormous whales to smaller seals, marine mammals have come to thrive in the cold waters of the Antarctic and are a key part of the area's food web. Marine mammals around the world, however, are facing serious threats from many sources. Climate change is rapidly affecting the seas they depend on for food and life. Pollution is making those seas less healthy to live in as well. The good news is that the animals' worldwide popularity has led to a huge increase in attention being paid by scientists and the general public alike. Conservation movements, including some discussed in Chapter 4, are helping to slow the decline of some species. Whether humans can repair the damage they've done to the ocean environment remains to be seen in the decades ahead. The answer will decide the fate of marine mammals.

 # Text-Dependent Questions:

1. What is baleen?
2. How did crabeater seals get their name?
3. What is another name for killer whales?

 # Research Project

Look more into killer whales. Find out where else they live besides the Antarctic and plot some of the largest populations on a world map.

Is this emperor penguin chick saying thanks? It probably should, after its dad spent months in freezing weather protecting the egg.

Penguins

Words to Understand

gait   the form and steps of how an animal walks

insulate   protect from heat or cold by padding or covering

regurgitate   spit up from the stomach

Is there a better-known bird in the world than the penguin? Several popular penguin movies, both fictional and documentary, have made world headlines. Penguins are found on just about any commercial product you can think of and stand as the logo for a publishing company, a professional hockey team, men's wear, pens, and many more. Their unique status as a flightless bird along with their comical way of walking sets them apart and above most other bird species. And, of course, there is a Batman villain named for them. The inspirations for all of those symbols and logos all live below the Antarctic Circle and even on the continent itself.

Penguin Basics

There are 18 species of penguins, all but one of which lives below the Antarctic Circle. There are no penguins at the North Pole or in the Arctic. Indeed, they are flightless birds, with a body better shaped for swimming than flying. Their wings and feet act as flippers, and they are able to move quickly and easily through the water. They survive in the icy cold of the southern seas thanks to a combination of feathers and fat. Their feathers are arranged in such as way as to make them a waterproof shield,

Penguins do not move well on land. Their familiar waddling gait has led to millions of funny videos. Sometimes penguins slide on their bellies, a behavior called tobogganing.

These African penguins, who also live on islands near Antarctica, show off their sleek swimming skills. Wings and flippers act as swim fins.

protecting the penguin's body from most of the cold. Under their skin and feathers, most species have a layer of fat that further **insulates** them.

Penguins live on fish and other small animals in the sea. They do nearly all their feeding while swimming. Emperor penguins can dive deeper than other penguin species, as much as 1,000 feet (300 m) under the sea. Some have been measured at staying under for more than 20 minutes. The female uses this deep-diving skill to fatten up and store a large amount of food. Other species can't dive as deep, but can move with amazing speed.

Surprise! This gentoo penguin will quickly be making a U-turn back into the water after hopping up on a floe already occupied by its deadly enemy.

Penguin predators include leopard seals and killer whales. The birds are at risk mostly in the water. But even resting on the ice can be a danger zone. Seals and whales have developed ways to break through ice and plunge the penguins back into the water, where they can be chased.

The Amazing Emperor

Penguins, like all birds, lay eggs. Most penguin species mate for life and will have many eggs in their lifetime. They usually only lay one egg at a time, however, and nearly all species return to the same nesting grounds year after year. For some birds, that's just a short hop to a nearby island. Others, however, have evolved to have a more difficult breeding process.

The emperor penguin has one of the most extreme journeys. Emperors are the largest species of penguin, at 60–80 pounds (30–40 kg) and 3–4 feet (1–1.2 m) tall. Their breeding colonies are also large, including tens of thousands of birds. One colony has been estimated at more than 200,000. These colony sites can be dozens—even more than 100 miles—from the open ocean. In the early Antarctic winter (April or May), the animals make the journey from the ocean to the breeding grounds to lay the egg.

In the months after hatching, emperor penguin families stay together with the chicks. They use smell and sounds to identify their own young.

Then the females head back to the water to feed. While they feed, they leave the males to stand in the biting winds and sub-freezing temperatures, protecting the egg. Male emperors stand for weeks at a time with the egg on their feet to keep it off of the ice. Thousands of them huddle together to share their warmth. When the females finally return as many as four months later, the egg has hatched and both the baby and father are starving. The mother **regurgitates** some of the food to feed her family.

The emperor penguin family unit has gained worldwide attention. The devotion of the father and the hard work of the mother has been featured in documentary films.

After the chick hatches and grows, the parents lead it back to the sea, where it will start the cycle again on its own.

All emperor penguins have their colonies on sea ice. The future of that behavior is threatened, however, and with it the existence of these remarkable birds. Ongoing climate change diminishes the amount of sea ice that forms each winter, which is when the birds breed. A 2014 report on one colony showed that within 50 years, the ice where they breed would be reduced by half.

The emperor chick will lose its grey feathers and grow black and white ones.

Satellites are helping to find out more about emperor penguins. They helped reveal the bad news about the reduction of the sea ice. They also showed, in a 2013 report, that there are twice as many birds as had been previously thought. The pictures taken from space showed nearly 600,000 total emperor penguins, almost double the earlier estimates.

That good news does not outweigh the issue of climate change, however, and many groups are working to have the emperor penguin put on the Endangered Species List.

Species Report

Adelie penguins have only black and white feathers and make their nests on rocky areas.

The only other penguin species that spends part of its year on the actual Antarctic mainland is the Adélie. This smaller penguin (27 inches/70 cm tall) got its name from the wife of a French explorer, Jules Dumont d'Urville, in the 1840s. Adélies are easily spotted by the white ring of feathers around each eye. They breed in spring, the reverse season from the emperors, making nests in rocky areas on the mainland or on nearby islands. The mating pair typically mates for life, and both male and female take part in caring for the egg and feeding the young penguins.

Chinstrap penguins take their name from the band of black feathers under what would be their chin. They live mostly on islands near Antarctica, such as South Georgia. One of the most abundant species of penguins, they are well known for their ability to toboggan. That means that sometimes on land they will lie on their stomachs and slide along the ice for a distance. As their walking **gait** is not that efficient, tobogganing is a better and faster way to get around!

Because the gentoo penguins breed on islands farther north from Antarctica, they have been a target of some human hunters over the years. However, efforts to reduce penguin hunting have greatly increased their numbers. Gentoo penguins have an orange bill and a white feather ring around each eye. They eat fish, including rock cod, as well as krill.

King penguins, nearly as large as emperors, are another species that has rebounded from human hunting. In

Penguin Scales

Australian scientists have learned a lot about one group of Adelie penguins near their Mawson research station. A colony of more than 1,800 pairs of Adelies breeds nearby. The scientists set up an Automated Penguin Monitoring System to help them keep track of some individual birds. The birds have had microchips implanted safely under their skin. As the birds walk over a platform placed between their colony and the sea, the machines identify and weigh each animal. The data can then be gathered to see how that weight changes over time or from season to season, as well as to have a headcount of birds in the colony.

A gentoo penguin is recognized by the bright orange bill and mouth parts.

the 19th century, they were a source of food and oil for far-ranging European and American whalers and fishermen. In the 20th century, though, such hunting fell off and king penguin numbers are healthy again.

This is a colony of king penguins, but you could also use the term "waddle."

South Georgia Site

The king penguins make for a particularly memorable sight on South Georgia Island. Located about 800 miles north of Antarctica, it is the closest piece of land with year-round human habitation. It's also an enormously popular spot for penguins, especially the king. At breeding season in the southern summer, more than 300,000 breeding pairs pack the island. Their squawks and calls can be heard for miles. They make a black-and-white blanket along some shores, with so many birds in one place that newcomers can't find a place to come ashore.

Macaroni penguins are also mostly black and white, but also have distinctive colored feathers on their head, along with bright orange bills and reddish-orange feet. They stand about 2.3 feet (70 cm) tall and only weigh about 13 pounds (6 kg). They make their homes on islands around Antarctica, but will visit the seas closer to the continent in search of their fish diet. Macaronis are unique among penguins in that they lay two eggs each breeding season.

Thanks to movies and popular culture, penguins are beloved animals around the world. They have been hit less hard by climate change and other human-caused problems. Some species on the Antarctic islands are thriving, while others, mostly on the continent, are doing less well. Scientists are carefully watching all these colonies in an effort to hold off any long-term problems with these sometimes-comical birds.

 # Text-Dependent Questions:

1. How do emperor penguins feed their babies?
2. What is "tobogganing"?
3. Why can penguins stay safely warm in icy waters?

 # Research Project

Here's a fun one: Watch one of the well-known penguin movies (*Happy Feet, Penguins of Madagascar,* or *Surf's Up,* for example) and see if you can spot places where the filmmakers took liberties with penguin behaviors—besides the fact that penguins can't talk, dance, or surf!

See baby emperor penguins in this PBS special

The majestic albatross can soar for days or even weeks without ever touching land. Its world-record wingspan is perfect for this soaring behavior.

In the Air . . . Under the Sea

3

Words to Understand

avian   relating to birds

crevice   a narrow crack or split, usually in rock

dehydrate   remove the water from

invertebrates   animals without skeletons or spines

nematodes   a worm-like invertebrate

prevalent   very common, abundant

Marine mammals get most of the headlines for Antarctic wildlife. Penguins also draw enormous attention. But there are other animals in the seas nearby and even on the land itself—the continent and nearby islands—that are drawing the attention of scientists and lovers of wildlife. All these birds and fish have had to adapt, like the penguins and marine mammals, to the harsh conditions.

The Mighty Albatross

The bird with the largest wingspan in the world calls the Antarctic region home. More than 20 species of albatross make their home on islands around the continental landmass. The most well-known is the largest, the wandering albatross. For centuries, sailors have marveled at this bird's ability to stay in the air for hours or days at a time. (An ancient sea story says that albatrosses carry with them the spirits of dead sailors. It was generally considered very bad luck to kill one.) Its wingspan of up to 11 feet (3.4 m) is the largest in the **avian** world. Albatrosses use their wide wings to glide on wind currents, sometimes going hours without flapping once.

They are large birds, weighing as much as 22 pounds (10 kg). They mate for life, making nests high on cliff faces in the Prince Edward Islands and other islands nearby. This height helps them take off easily, since their large size and wide wingspan makes running on land for takeoff difficult. They lay an egg and raise only one chick per year, during the Southern Hemisphere summer in December and January. This low birth rate is one reason their numbers are falling. Deaths from being caught in fishing longlines is another; many of the albatross species are considered threatened or endangered.

They are caught in those lines, which drag from behind moving fishing boats, because their diet is fish. They swoop down to eat fish near the surface. Fishing boats, however, throw dead fish and fish parts overboard, so the albatrosses often see them

A gathering of albatrosses flocks together near a nesting site on an island near the Antarctic continent. Albatrosses mate for life.

as a source of an easy meal. They fly down and are snagged and dragged under by the lines. Many countries are trying to pass laws against using such lines, or at least to get fishing boats to use methods that don't endanger albatrosses and other sea birds.

On the Wing

While albatrosses are part of seafaring lore, the skua bird gets no such respect. This fierce scavenger has a reputation for being a thief and a killer. Penguin eggs are one of its favored foods, and the nearly defenseless penguin parents can often do little to stop a skua raid. Skuas can also sometimes take penguin chicks. Skuas also are famous for stealing fish from other birds, such as gulls or petrels. Visitors to skua colonies report being "buzzed" by adult skuas if the visitor strays too close to a nest. With a wingspan of 4.5 feet (140 cm) or so, they are large birds, they are fast, and have sharp claws and a beak with a hook that they use to grab prey.

Another Antarctic bird holds the title of southernmost breeder. The snowy petrel will sometimes lay its summer eggs on the Antarctic continent itself. Sightings of the snowy petrel at the South Pole itself have been reported. It has completely snowy white feathers and is about the size of a pigeon. Its mating ritual is an amazing aerial display. Females lead males on a fast-moving mid-air ballet, perhaps to check the strength and flying skills of their potential mates. Once they have mated, they look for rocky **crevices** or covered ledges to lay their eggs. They protect their eggs from raiding skuas—and approaching tourists with cameras—by vomiting up a stinky stream of digested food. They are beautiful birds, but don't get too close!

The Arctic tern is a bird that really does not like winter. These birds undertake one of the longest migrations of any animal in the world. After breeding in the Arctic in the spring (April or May), they fly with their young all the way south to enjoy the Antarctic summer (November to February, approximately). Tracking gear put on the birds by scientists has shown annual migration distances of more than 50,000 miles (80,000 km) in the air for some birds. About a foot long, they have a distinctive forked tail.

Loud and fearless, the skua bird is the pirate raider of the Antarctic. Skua birds often take penguin eggs or even small chicks as prey.

The blue-eyed shag is a type of cormorant, a diving bird. Blue-eyed shags live on islands near Antarctica, gathering in huge breeding colonies on rocky shores and cliffs. As their name says, they have bright blue eyes. These shags also have a bumpy clump of yellow-orange tissue on their beaks that grows over time. Shags like to stick together. They rarely will nest alone, but always with huge flocks of other shags. Even when hunting fish,

The reason for the name of the blue-eyed shag is readily apparent in this closeup. Given their foul aroma, it's just as well this image is not scratch-and-sniff.

they work in packs, floating in a large "raft" rather than feeding individually. Among workers on South Atlantic islands, shags are well known for their powerful and distinctive smell, too. One small island where they nest in large numbers is even named Shagnasty Island.

Permanent Residents

Unlike the fish and marine mammals that live in the Antarctic waters, a small group of tiny **invertebrates** makes the land-mass their home. The largest animal living year-round on Ant-arctica is a midge called *Belgica antarctica*. It's less than 1 mm (0.03 in) long. The midge is joined by a handful of tiny, worm-like **nematodes** and a few even smaller springtails, which are hard-shelled animals related to insects. They don't live in or on the ice, but instead find those few places where rock or soil clings to the continent.

Midges live mostly in clumps of moss that grow seasonally. Other tiny creatures live near season bird nests. They live on the plants such as moss, algae, and lichen that grow during short spans of time when the weather warms slightly. But what do they do the rest of the year?

Survival in the dry, sub-freezing temperatures of the Antarc-tic winter is a huge challenge. These little animals have evolved several processes that let them make it through. Most of them are able to go into a type of deep hibernation. Their bodies are able to reach sub-zero temperatures but still recover. Unlike

This is one of the largest full-time animal residents of Antarctica. The tiny midge can enter a long state of hibernation to survive freezing winters.

most animals, when the water in their body freezes, it does not damage their tissues. Another strategy some employ is to **dehydrate** almost completely. That way, there is little water in their bodies to freeze. They hibernate in this state until water melts. It's somewhat like a dry sponge, growing and coming back to "life" when water is added.

Scientists are studying these amazing creatures with an eye toward outer space. Can these midges give clues about how life can exist in other challenging environments and habitats?

Fish in the Sea

The most **prevalent** species of sea creature around Antarctica is also the way that many other sea and land creatures survive. Krill are tiny, shrimp-like crustaceans. They live by the hundreds of

The large eyes and multiple legs of the krill show its relationship to the shrimp family. Krill are the key prey species for dozens of animals in the Antarctic.

At the Bottom

At the edges of the Antarctic landmass is an undersea continental shelf. This is a wide area of undersea land in shallow waters. At its edges, the land stops and the depth of the water plunges to thousands of feet. On that shelf, though, is a crowded ecosystem called a benthic community. That means it's a group of animals that live together on the bottom of the ocean. In the Antarctic, such creatures include sponges, mollusks, crustaceans, and nematodes. Because the waters are so rich with plant plankton, the Antarctic species of some of these grow much larger than in other parts of the world. It's a dark and cold but very active place for wildlife near Antarctica.

millions in the cold waters of the South Atlantic. Some species of whales, seals, birds, and fish of all kinds depend on krill for a large part of their diet. About two inches (6 cm) long, they play a role in this ecosystem much larger than their physical size.

The waters of the Antarctic are a great breeding ground for these animals. They eat the massive amounts of phytoplankton (tiny ocean plants) that rise from the bottom of the sea. Because krill mostly live near the surface of the water, the year-round sun in the summer provides heat energy. It's a good thing they have such fertile breeding grounds, since so many of them are eaten each year. Krill mass in groups numbering in the millions of pounds. One estimate said that krill on Earth (they live in other places besides the Antarctic, too) might outweigh all humans put together. Some scientists think that the particular Antarctic krill species (there are more than 80 species of krill) might have more animals than any other single species in the world.

As successful at breeding as krill are, some studies show their numbers declining. All signs point to the warming oceans caused by climate change. This is particularly worrying because of the huge numbers of other animals that depend on krill to survive. A falloff in krill population could have a domino effect through the ecosystem.

Krill are not the only fish in the Antarctic sea. The mackerel icefish is one of the most unique looking. These fish do not have the chemicals in their body that color their blood, so it gives them

In the icy depths of the Antarctic waters, amazing icefish don't need much color. They are nearly transparent; the color blob here shows its internal organs.

The next stop for this massive toothfish is probably someone's dinner table. Marketed as Chilean sea bass, the toothfish is facing overfishing in Antarctic waters.

a ghostly appearance. They rest near the bottom, then come back toward the surface to feed.

You or your family might very well have eaten another Antarctic fish, but because of good marketing, you might not know it. Since the late 1980s, Chilean sea bass have regularly appeared at markets and on menus in the US, Canada, and Europe. Those fish are not from Chile and are not bass. In fact, they are either Antarctic or Patagonian toothfish. A fisherman changed the name of the toothfish before selling it, and the "friendlier" name led to a huge surge in demand. Huge stocks of them have been fished, almost to the point of overfishing. About 6–7 feet (1.8–2.1 m) long, the toothfish lives on the bottom of the cold seas. Interest has fallen a bit, and fishing stocks are being more carefully monitored to make sure the species will survive well.

Text-Dependent Questions:

1. What is the most prevalent sea species of the Antarctic region?

2. What is the continent's largest land animal?

3. What bird steals penguin eggs?

Research Project

Do online research about the Antarctic food web. To show the importance of krill, make a poster that shows the web from the bottom up.

Deep undersea life around Antarctica

How long will human animals be able to see the eerily beautiful Antarctic scenery? Ongoing climate change and other human actions are a growing threat.

Protecting Antarctic Wildlife

4

Words to Understand

fossil fuels   gas, oil, and natural gas, all of which come from the decayed remains of long-ago animals

invasive species   animals that are not native to a region but are introduced with negative consequences

moratorium   a temporary ban of an action

toxic   poisonous

The animals that live at the bottom of the world have a tough enough life without people coming along to make it harder. Because of human actions, life in the Antarctic is changing for some animals. However, those changes are not coming as quickly or as terribly as they are for animals in other parts of the world. Human activities are threatening tens of thousands of species, from magnificent elephants to tiny insects. So far, similar impacts are muted in the Antarctic, but scientists and conservationists are working hard to try to prevent any further negative impacts.

Threat of Climate Change

The major issue facing all wildlife around the world is ongoing global climate change. Thanks to humanity's vast use of **fossil fuels** in the past century, the atmosphere of the planet is trapping more and more heat. That is leading to very tiny annual increases in temperature that have added up to a global crisis. The delicate balance of nature and the environment is changing as the Earth warms. For a land of ice like Antarctica, this can be disastrous. As the air warms, the ocean warms. As the ocean warms, it melts the Antarctic ice at a faster rate than before.

For example, one of the fastest-warming areas in the world is the West Antarctica ice sheet. If, over time, that ice sheet were to melt, it contains enough water to raise world ocean levels by more than 100 feet. That would inundate coastal areas worldwide. That's bad news for humans, of course, but cataclysmic for animal species. Many animals depend on the ice sheets and other areas of Antarctic ice to survive. Even the key to the food web, krill, eat the algae on the bottom of some ice sheets.

Ongoing threats to marine wildlife in Antarctica

Another aspect of climate change is the growth of carbon dioxide (CO_2) in the atmosphere. That also is a result of the massive use of fuels in the 20th century and today. The destruction of CO_2-absorbing plant life has made this problem even worse. The southern oceans around Antarctica, scientists believe, will start

When a large piece of a glacier breaks off and falls into the sea, the action is called "calving." Reducing the size of glaciers is a dangerous part of climate change.

to face greater and greater threat from this gas, which is partly absorbed by ocean water. However, the chemical balance of that water would be thrown off by too much CO_2. That means trouble for any fish species that depends on that water for life. Again, make a change in the food web by reducing fish population and you affect every animal connected to those fish.

The issue of how to address climate change globally is one of the most important facing humanity. Governments around the

The snowy petrel, here making its way through its namesake, is among the animals that will benefit from the new Ross Sea Marine Protected Area.

world signed an agreement in 2016 to try to limit their use of fossil fuels in the years ahead. Whether that agreement will be enforced or will even be enough remains to be seen.

Creating a Safe Sea

Environmentalists have for years been calling on world governments to set aside key areas around Antarctica as Marine

Protected Areas. This would prevent development, as well as fishing and other human activities, that would harm wildlife. In 2016, the Commission for the Conservation of Antarctic Marine Living Resources (CCAMLR) agreed to designate the Ross Sea as an MPA. The key was a Russian agreement to the document; that nation had long been a holdout. Because of the agreement, 24 nations will not take anything from the Ross Sea MPA for 35 years. This will have long-lasting positive effects on Adélie penguins, krill, snowy petrels, and many other animal species.

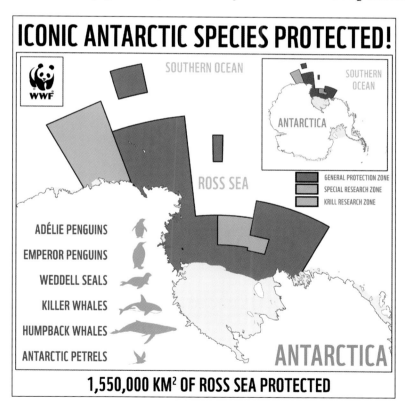

This graphic provided by the World Wildlife Fund shows the extent of the Ross Sea MPA, as well as some of the animals that will be positively affected.

"I'm absolutely overjoyed," said Lewis Pugh, the UN patron for the oceans. "[With an area three times the size of Texas,] this is the biggest protected area on the land or the sea, is the first large scale MPA on the high seas."

Groups such as the Antarctic and Southern Ocean Coalition are working hard to have other areas near Antarctica declared MPAs and help even more animals.

Stopping Illegal Whaling

Whales used to number in the millions around the world, with the Southern Ocean being one of their favored feeding grounds. A demand for whale oil in the 18th and 19th centuries, however,

Humpbacks were once among the key targets of whalers. Another species, the right whale in the Northern Hemisphere, was almost hunted to extinction.

This Japanese whaling ship is one of many still taking several species of whales. They say they are for research, but international groups doubt that claim.

saw whale populations plummet as whale hunters killed these valuable animals by the thousands. With the arrival of electricity, whales were partly spared and began to come back in numbers. However, new threats arose from modern-day hunters looking for whale meat and from other types of fishing that negatively affected whales.

In 1982, the International Whaling Commission (IWC) put a **moratorium**—a temporary ban—on whaling in the Southern Ocean. In 1994, the IWC made it permanent, declaring the entire

Invaders!

The birds and small mammals that live on the Antarctic islands have few land predators. The most dangerous are **invasive species** introduced to the islands. Until sailing ships arrived, there were no rats or mice on the islands. But stowaways on those ships ended up onshore and have since multiplied and caused damage to native plants and animals. Insects that have arrived via human travel have also caused problems.

On the Antarctic continent itself, crabs might be the next invasive species. A type of king crab seems to be slowly moving closer to the continent, braving waters that were once too cold for it. Scientists are also carefully watching tourists to make sure they don't accidentally bring in invasive species of plants or animals.

area around Antarctica as the Southern Ocean Whale Sanctuary. This meant that whalers were no longer legally allowed to track and kill whales in this area. Private groups like Sea Shepherd, as well as government agencies, enforce this ban. Some countries, though—notably Japan—continue to hunt there, though in smaller numbers than in the past. Japan says that its kills fall under the ban's "scientific killing" rules that allow for a limited number of whales to be taken to learn more about all whales. However, Japan only takes useful minke whales, so their claims are hotly disputed.

Overall, the international work seems to have helped the whales of the Southern Oceans, but more study is needed.

Studying (and Cleaning Up)

Finding out more about how animals in the Antarctic live and survive will go a long way to making sure their homes are kept safe in the future. Antarctica is home to several major year-round science stations. The United States operates facilities at Ross Island (McMurdo Station); at the geographic South Pole

(Amundsen-Scott South Pole Station); and on Anvers Island in the Antarctic Peninsula region (Palmer Station). Scientists from many disciplines spend time at each focusing on their specialty, all working under the National Science Foundation and the United States Antarctic Program. The international Antarctic Wildlife

On the shores of the Ross Sea—and hemmed in by sea ice for long stretches in the winter—the McMurdo Research Station is home to hundreds of scientists.

Cruise ships like this one visiting pristine Antarctic waters are a growing controversy. Will they do more harm than good? Is bringing tourists to Antarctica worth the risk?

Research Fund focuses on animal research, sending scientists to those and other stations.

All those scientific visitors take care not to add their own harm to the wildlife and environment. The first human visitors to Antarctica had a different approach and only rarely cleaned up after themselves. Passing ships and temporary science stations left behind garbage dumps of human refuse and trash. Current human visitors, however, are learning to take better care of their temporary homes. There are strict rules, too, about dumping pollution or **toxic** liquids into the waters around Antarctica.

Can Visitors Help?

Inviting visitors to such a beautiful place is a mixed blessing. Tourism to the Antarctic continues to rise each year. In the 1980s, perhaps a couple of thousand people made the dangerous journey to this forbidding place. In recent years, annual numbers have jumped to nearly 40,000. A wide variety of tours takes visitors to see penguins, seals, whales, and more. There are even skydiving adventures and airplane sightseeing trips over the South Pole.

On Antarctica and several nearby islands, tourists can get up close and personal with animals such as penguins, many of whom have not come to fear human contact yet.

Only a trained scientist should attempt this sort of close approach to a roaring elephant seal. A group of king penguins is on the sidelines for the encounter.

The increase in visitors might have a negative impact on the area and on wildlife. More people means more trash. Visitors have to get there in boats powered by fuel and oil, which can spill and kill wildlife. The ships also put out CO_2, adding to the global issue. Once ashore, not every tour operator is diligent about keeping people and wildlife separate and safe. There is also an occasional need for dangerous and expensive rescues of stranded ships or visitors.

On the plus side, many experts feel that the exposure to the amazing sights and incredible wildlife of the continent can help conservation efforts. By having more and more people actually experience the Antarctic, efforts to preserve it and conserve wildlife will have new allies and support. Cruise ships are trying to get closer and closer to Antarctica, as environmental groups and scientists watch carefully. The key in the future will be to find the right balance.

From tiny midges to enormous blue whales, from soaring albatrosses to deep-diving seals, the Antarctic has an amazing variety of animals able to survive its cold environment. Whether they will have that environment in the future depends on how people learn to understand what they are doing to the world and how they can change to reduce the negative impacts. Protecting penguins and whales seems like a small thing globally, but it all adds up. We are all connected.

 # Text-Dependent Questions:

1. What is an MPA?
2. What did the IWC ban in 1994?
3. What happens at McMurdo Sound?

 # Research Project

Go online and find an online diary kept by one of the scientists stationed in Antarctica. See if you can find contact information and send them questions about what it is like to survive as a human animal in such challenging conditions.

FIND OUT MORE

Websites

www.coolantarctica.com/
From animals to tourism, from history to gear, this site has everything about Antarctica.

www.asoc.org/index.php
The Antarctic and Southern Ocean Coalition gathers a host of information about conservation of animals and the environment.

www.antarctica.gov.au/
Learn more about all the animals in this book at this site run by the Australian government's Antarctic Division.

Books

Kavanagh, James. *Antarctic Wildlife: A Folding Pocket Guide*. Dunedin, FL: Waterford Press, 2013.

Lowen, James. *Antarctic Wildlife: A Visitor's Guide*. Princeton, NJ: Princeton University Press, 2011.

Taylor, Barbara. *Eyewitness: Arctic and Antarctica*. New York: DK Publishing, 2012.

SERIES GLOSSARY OF KEY TERMS

circumpolar: the area surrounding the North Pole, including the Arctic regions

Cold War: when nations are openly hostile toward each other while not resorting to physical warfare

continental shelf: the relatively shallow seabed surrounding a continent; the edge of a continent as it slopes down into the sea

floe: an ice sheet floating in the water

indigenous: native or original to a particular place

meterology: the study of weather

pelts: furred animal skins

permafrost: a layer of soil that stays frozen all year long

province: an area in Canada with its own name and government, similar to a state

subsistence: a basic, minimal way of living, with only things that are necessary to survive

sustainable: something that can be maintained or practiced for a long duration without negative effects

taiga: a biome that includes the forest of mostly evergreen trees found in the southern Arctic regions

territorial waters: the parts of an ocean over which a country has control

tundra: a type of biome in very cold areas characterized by limited plant growth, frozen soil, and low rainfall

INDEX

PHOTO CREDITS

ABOUT THE AUTHOR
James Buckley Jr. is the author of many books about animals and nature. He wrote the *Animal Planet Animal Atlas*, Discovery's *Snakeopedia* and *Bugopedia*, and contributed to the *Animals: A Visual Encyclopedia*. He also wrote books for DK Publishing and Boys' Life about nature, the outdoors, fishing, and more. He lives in Santa Barbara, California, which is much warmer than the Antarctic.